What Makes a Town?

Diana Kenney, M.A.Ed., NBCT

Consultants

Shelley Scudder
Gifted Education Teacher
Broward County Schools

Caryn Williams, M.S.Ed.
Madison County Schools
Huntsville, AL

Publishing Credits

Dona Herweck Rice, *Editor-in-Chief*

Lee Aucoin, *Creative Director*

Torrey Maloof, *Editor*

Diana Kenney, M.A.Ed., NBCT,
Associate Education Editor

Marissa Rodriguez, *Designer*

Stephanie Reid, *Photo Editor*

Rachelle Cracchiolo, M.S.Ed., *Publisher*

Teacher Created Materials

5301 Oceanus Drive
Huntington Beach, CA 92649-1030
http://www.tcmpub.com

ISBN 978-1-4333-6969-8

© 2014 Teacher Created Materials, Inc.

Table of Contents

A Place to Live

Some people live in small towns. Some people live in big towns. Big towns are called **cities**. People all live in **communities** (kuh-MYOO-ni-teez). Communities are places where groups of people live and work together.

This is a big city.

This is a house in a small town.

Helping Hands

People in towns help one another. Firefighters put out fires. They save people. Police officers make sure people follow the **laws**. Laws keep people safe.

Police officers also keep us safe on the road.

Buckets of Water

When there was a fire in the **past**, people would form a long line. They would pass buckets of water to the fire or fire hose. It did not work very well.

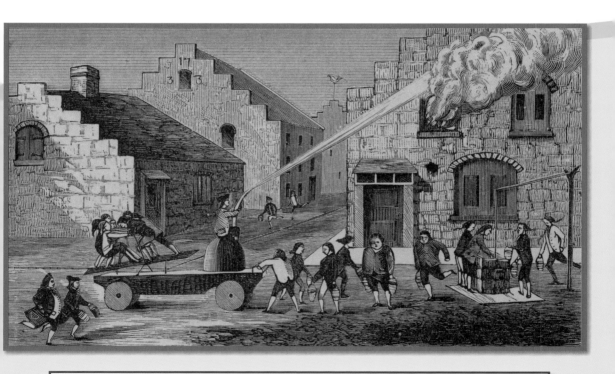

People carry buckets of water to the fire hose long ago.

Doctors help people stay well. In the past, doctors went to see people. Today, people go to see doctors.

Teachers help kids learn. In the past, teachers had chalk and books. In the **present**, teachers have many types of **tools**.

A teacher writes on a chalkboard in 1899.

A New Kind of Board

Some schools no longer have chalkboards. They have special whiteboards. People can write on them with their fingers or a special pen.

A student writes on a whiteboard today.

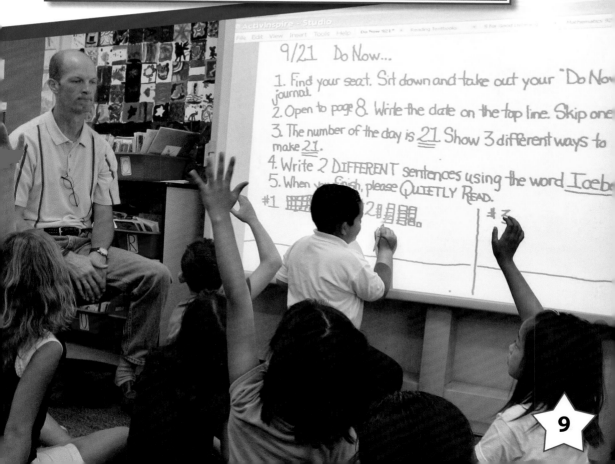

Places to Go

Towns are busy places. Most towns have a bank and a post office. There are stores where people can buy food. Towns even have places where people go to have fun!

Kids wait in line at a bank in 1925.

Disneyland

Disneyland is a fun place to go in Anaheim, California.

This is Disneyland today.

Transportation (trans-per-TEY-shuhn) helps people move from place to place. Long ago, people walked or rode horses. Today, they move in fast cars. They ride in buses. There are many ways for people to get where they are going.

A man uses a horse to get around long ago.

Today, many people use buses and cars.

Ways to Stay in Touch

It is important for people in towns to **communicate** (kuh-MYOO-ni-keyt) with one another. When people communicate, they talk to other people. They may talk about their kids. They may talk about the news.

These people talk at a fair in 1938.

These people talk while they walk.

People in towns communicate in many ways. In the past, people wrote letters. They read newspapers. Today, people can use computers. They can send emails to their friends. They can read news online.

Some people read the news on their cell phones.

Snail Mail

A letter that is mailed at the post office is called *snail mail*. It takes more time to reach the other person than an email does.

A woman puts a letter in a mailbox in 1910.

Home

A town is more than just a place to live and work. It is more than stores and parks. It is a community of people who help one another. It is a place to call home.

These kids play together in 1941.

These kids play together today.

Find It!

Ask an adult to help you explore your town. Look for things and people that make your town special. Try to find everything on the list below!

Try to find a:

- ✓ bus
- ✓ car
- ✓ doctor
- ✓ firefighter
- ✓ mailbox
- ✓ newspaper
- ✓ police officer
- ✓ post office
- ✓ store
- ✓ teacher

This girl explores her town.

Glossary

cities—big towns where people live and work

communicate—to give information about something to someone else

communities—places where groups of people live and work together

laws—a set of rules made by a government

past—an earlier time

present—the period of time that is now

tools—things that are used to do a job

transportation—a way of moving from place to place

Index

Your Turn!

Fun and Games

The kids in this photo from 1941 like to play games. Draw a picture or write a list of games you like to play in your town.